JUST FOR FUN

CHRISTMAS MANDOLIN

MORE THAN 40 CHRISTMAS CLASSICS

Produced by
Alfred Music Publishing Co., Inc.
P.O. Box 10003
Van Nuys, CA 91410-0003
alfred.com

Printed in USA.

ISBN-10: 0-7390-6974-8
ISBN-13: 978-0-7390-6974-5

Cover Photos
Central image models: Katrina Hruschka and Andrew Callahan / Photographer: Brian Immke, www.adeptstudios.com
Mandolin: courtesy of Gibson USA • Sleigh: © istockphoto / Golkin Oleg • Christmas ornaments: © istockphoto / jammydesign
Background doodles: copyright Elise Gravel, 2009, used under license from Shutterstock.com

 Alfred Cares. Contents printed on 100% recycled paper.

HOW TO USE THIS BOOK

There are two rhythm options supplied for almost every song in this book. Rhythm Option 1 is an easy-level strum pattern that can be played through the song's chord changes, with the chord fingerings shown throughout the song. Rhythm Option 2 is an intermediate-level arrangement written in full notation and TAB. Option 2 often combines melody and accompaniment, making it perfect not only for accompanying a singer but also for solo performances for friends, family, and recitals. Plus, the melody for every song is written out in notation and TAB.

CONTENTS

ANGELS WE HAVE HEARD ON HIGH

TRADITIONAL FRENCH CAROL

Moderately

An - gels we have heard on high, sweet - ly sing - ing o'er the plains.

And the moun - tains in re - ply, ech - o - ing their joy - ous strains.

Angels We Have Heard on High - 2 - 1

AULD LANG SYNE

Words by
ROBERT BURNS

TRADITIONAL SCOTTISH AIR

Auld Lang Syne - 2 - 1

AWAY IN A MANGER
(Cradle Song)

TRADITIONAL WORDS

Music by
WILLIAM J. KIRKPATRICK

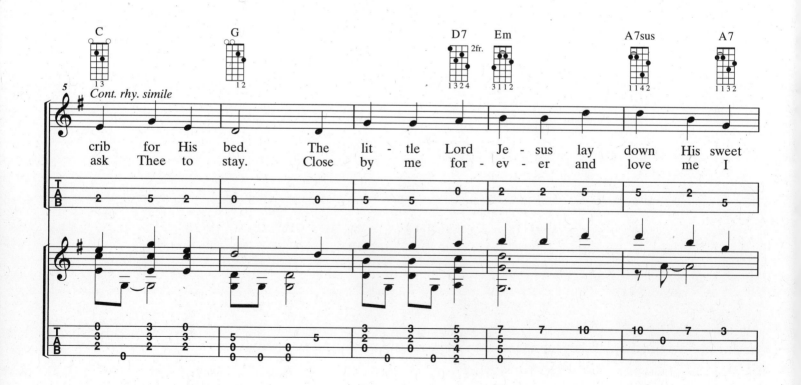

Away in a Manger - 3 - 1

BRING A TORCH, JEANNETTE, ISABELLA

TRADITIONAL FRENCH

Bring a Torch, Jeannette, Isabella - 3 - 1

Bring a Torch, Jeannette, Isabella - 3 - 3

14

AWAY IN A MANGER

TRADITIONAL WORDS

Music by
JAMES R. MURRAY

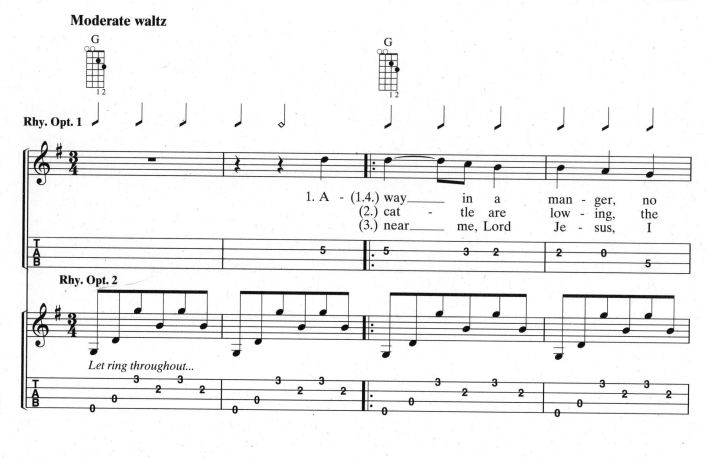

Away in a Manger - 2 - 1

CAROL OF THE BIRDS

TRADITIONAL

Verse 3:
Angels and shepherds, birds of the sky,
Come where the Son of God doth lie.
Christ on earth with man doth dwell,
Join in the shout, ÒNoel, Noel!Ó

Carol of the Birds - 2 - 2

A CHILD THIS DAY IS BORN

Verse 3:
And as the angel told them,
So to them did appear.
They found the young Child, Jesus Christ,
With Mary, his Mother dear.
(To Chorus:)

DANCE OF THE SUGAR PLUM FAIRY

Music by
PETER ILYICH TCHAIKOVSKY

Brightly

Mandolin Solo:

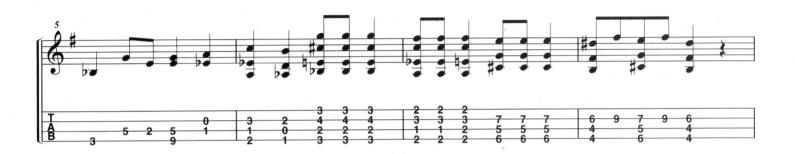

THE COVENTRY CAROL

TRADITIONAL ENGLISH

The Coventry Carol - 2 - 1

Verse 2:
O sisters too, how may we do,
For to preserve this day.
This poor youngling for whom we sing,
Bye, bye, lulloo, lullay.

Verse 3:
Herod the king in his raging,
Charged he hath this day.
His men of might, in his own sight,
All children young to slay.

Verse 4:
Then woe is me, poor Child, for thee,
And ever mourn and say.
For Thy parting nor say nor sing,
Bye, bye, lulloo, lullay.

DECK THE HALLS

TRADITIONAL CAROL

Deck the Halls - 2 - 2

THE FIRST NOEL

TRADITIONAL CAROL

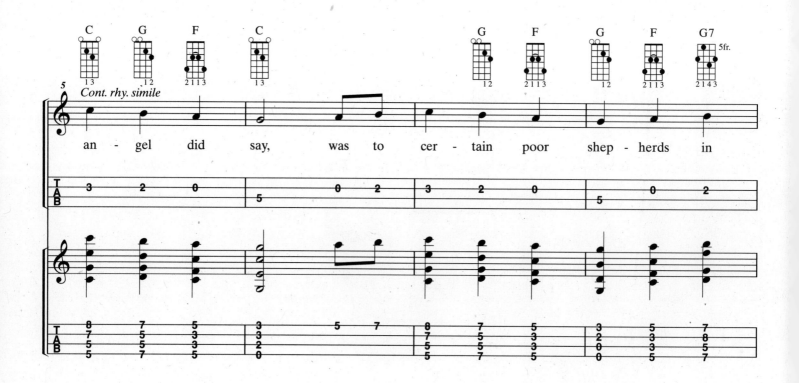

The First Noel - 3 - 1

The First Noel - 3 - 3

GO TELL IT ON THE MOUNTAIN

TRADITIONAL SPIRTUAL

Go Tell It on the Mountain - 2 - 1

Verse 3:
While shepherds kept their watching
O'er wand'ring flock by night,
Behold, from out the Heavens
There shown a holy light.
(To Chorus:)

Verse 4:
And lo, when they had seen it,
They all bowed down and prayed.
Then they travelled on together,
To where the Babe was laid.
(To Chorus:)

GOD REST YE MERRY, GENTLEMEN

TRADITIONAL ENGLISH CAROL

Brightly, with a bounce

1. God
rest you mer - ry, gen - tle - men, let noth - ing you dis - may. Re - and
God, our Heav'n - ly Fa - ther, a bless - ed an - gel came,

3.–7. See additional lyrics

God Rest Ye Merry, Gentlemen - 4 - 1

Verse 3:
In Bethlehem, in Jewry,
This Blessed Babe was born.
And laid within a manger
Upon this holy morn,
The which his Mother Mary
Did nothing take in scorn.
Oh, tidings...

Verse 4:
Fear not then, said the angel,
Let nothing you affright.
This day is born a Savior,
Of a pure Virgin bright,
To free all those who trust in Him
From SatanÕs power and might."
Oh, tidings...

Verse 5:
The shepherds at those tidings
Rejoiced much in mind,
And left their flocks a-feeding
In tempest, storm, and wind,
And went to Bethlehem straightway,
The Son of God to find.
Oh, tidings...

Verse 6:
And when they came to Bethlehem
Where our dear Savior lay,
They found Him in a manger
Where oxen feed on hay.
His Mother Mary kneeling down,
Unto the Lord did pray.
Oh, tidings...

Verse 7:
Now to the Lord sing praises,
All you within this place.
And with true love and brotherhood
Each other now embrace.
This holy tide of Christmas
All other doth deface.
Oh, tidings...

GOOD KING WENCESLAS

TRADITIONAL ENGLISH CAROL

Moderately

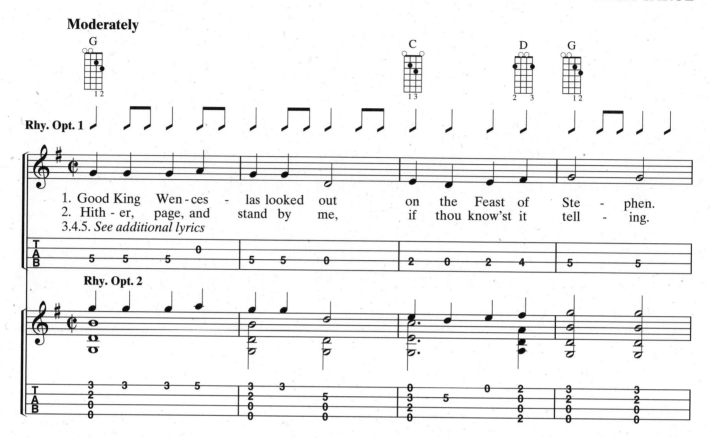

1. Good King Wen - ces - las looked out on the Feast of Ste - phen.
2. Hith - er, page, and stand by me, if thou know'st it tell - ing.
3.4.5. *See additional lyrics*

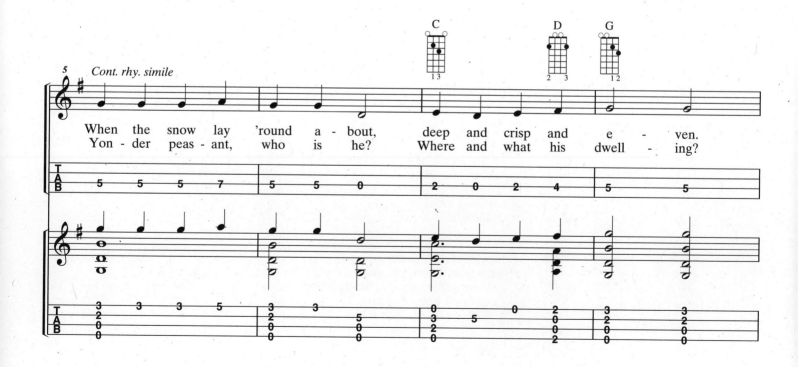

When the snow lay 'round a - bout, deep and crisp and e - ven.
Yon - der peas - ant, who is he? Where and what his dwell - ing?

Good King Wenceslas - 2 - 1

Verse 3:
"Bring me flesh and bring me wine, bring me pine logs hither.
Thou and I will see him dine, when we bear him thither."
Page and monarch forth they went, forth they went together,
Through the rude wind's wild lament and the bitter weather.

Verse 4:
"Sire, the night is darker now, and the wind blows stronger.
Fails my heart, I know not how, I can go no longer."
"Mark my footsteps, my good page, tread thou in them boldly.
Thou shalt find the winter's rage freeze thy blood less coldly."

Verse 5:
In his master's steps he trod, where the snow lay dinted.
Heat was in the very sod which the Saint had printed.
Therefore, Christian men, be sure, wealth or rank possessing;
Ye who will now bless the poor shall yourselves find blessing.

HARK! THE HERALD ANGELS SING

Words by
CHARLES WESLEY

Music by
FELIX MENDELSSOHN

Hark! The Herald Angels Sing - 3 - 1

Hark! The Herald Angels Sing - 3 - 2

Hark! The Herald Angels Sing - 3 - 3

HAVE YOURSELF A MERRY LITTLE CHRISTMAS

Words and Music by
HUGH MARTIN and RALPH BLANE

Have Yourself a Merry Little Christmas - 2 - 1

Have Yourself a Merry Little Christmas - 2 - 2

HERE WE COME A-WASSAILING

OLD ENGLISH

THE HOLLY AND THE IVY

TRADITIONAL

The Holly and the Ivy - 2 - 1

Verse 2:
The holly bears a blossom,
As white as lily flow'r,
And Mary bore sweet Jesus Christ
To be our sweet Savior.
(To Refrain:)

Verse 3:
The holly bears a berry,
As red as any blood,
And Mary bore sweet Jesus Christ
To do poor sinners good.
(To Refrain:)

HOLY NIGHT, PEACEFUL NIGHT

Words and Music by
SIR JOSEPH BARNBY

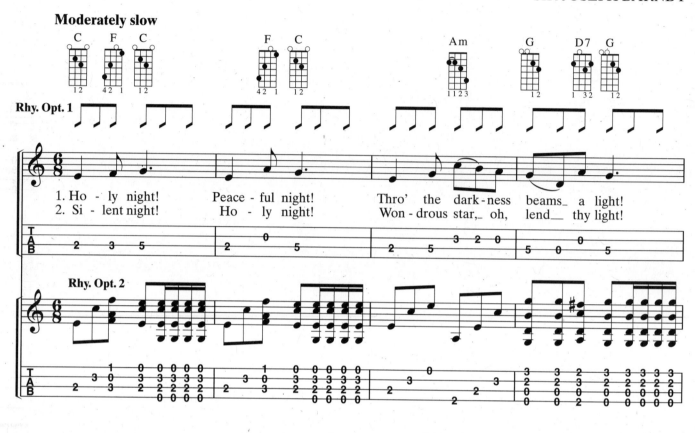

Holy Night, Peaceful Night - 2 - 1

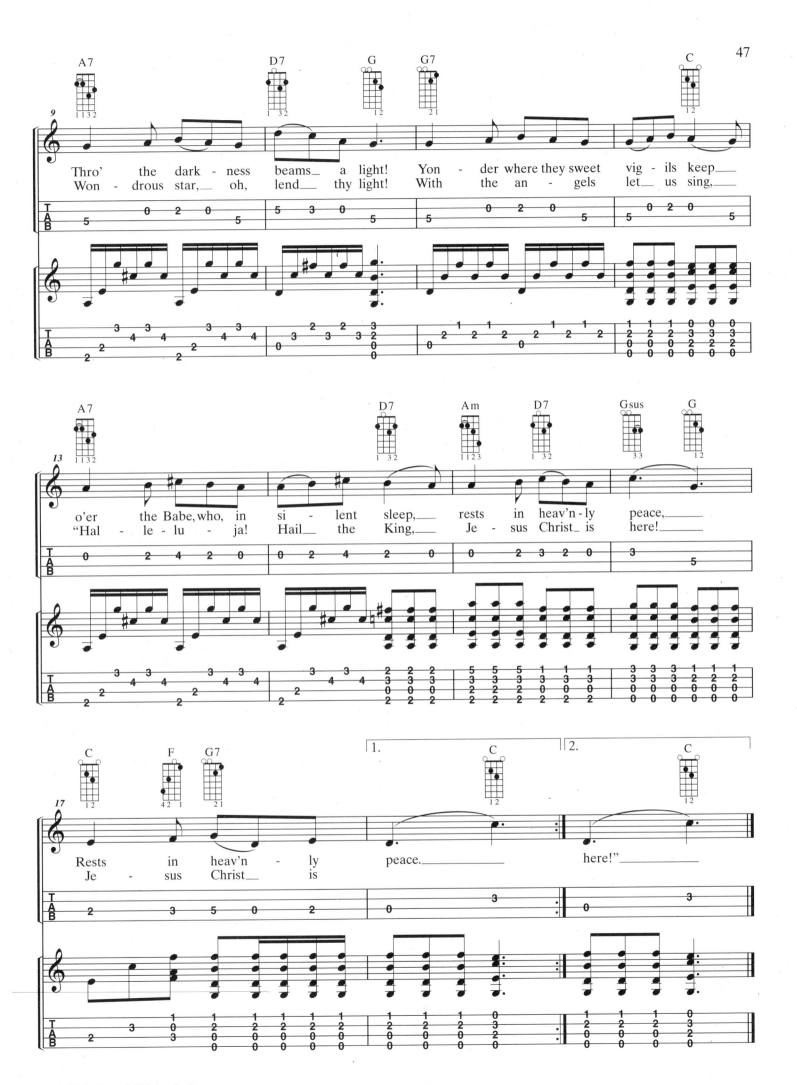

Holy Night, Peaceful Night - 2 - 2

I HEARD THE BELLS ON CHRISTMAS DAY

Words by
HENRY WADSWORTH LONGFELLOW

Music by
HENRY BISHOP

I Heard the Bells on Christmas Day - 2 - 1

I Heard the Bells on Christmas Day - 2 - 2

I SAW THREE SHIPS

TRADITIONAL

6.–9. *See additional lyrics*

Verse 6:
And all the bells on earth shall sing
On Christmas Day, On Christmas Day.
And all the bells on earth shall sing
On Christmas Day in the morning.

Verse 7:
And all the Angels in heaven shall sing
On Christmas Day, On Christmas Day.
And all the Angels in heaven shall sing
On Christmas Day in the morning.

Verse 8:
And all the souls on earth shall sing
On Christmas Day, On Christmas Day.
And all the souls on earth shall sing
On Christmas Day in the morning.

Verse 9:
Then let us all rejoice, amain,
On Christmas Day, On Christmas Day.
Then let us all rejoice, amen,
On Christmas Day in the morning.

IN THE BLEAK MIDWINTER

Words by
C. G. ROSSETTI

Music by
THOMAS B. STRONG

In the Bleak Midwinter - 2 - 1

IT CAME UPON THE MIDNIGHT CLEAR

Words by
RICHARD S. WILLIS

Music by
EDMUND H. SEARS

It Came Upon the Midnight Clear - 2 - 1

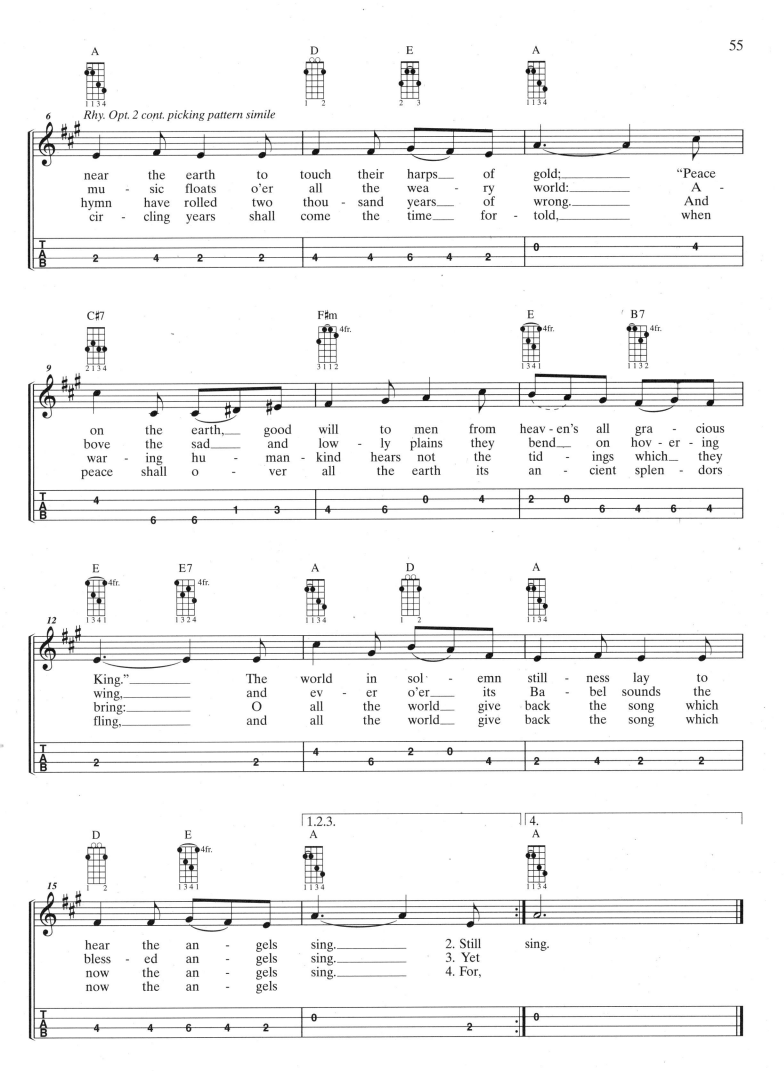

It Came Upon the Midnight Clear - 2 - 2

JESU, JOY OF MAN'S DESIRING

By
J.S. BACH

Moderately

Mandolin Solo:

Jesu, Joy of Man's Desiring - 2 - 1

Jesu, Joy of Man's Desiring - 2 - 2

JINGLE BELLS

Words and Music by
J. PIERPONT

Jingle Bells - 3 - 1

Verse:

1. Dash - ing through the snow in a one-horse, o - pen sleigh,
2.3. *See additional lyrics*

o'er the fields we go, laugh - ing all the way.

Bells on bob - tail ring, mak - ing spir - its bright; what

fun it is to ride and sing a sleigh - ing song to - night! Oh!

Jingle Bells - 3 - 2

Verse 2:
A day or two ago,
I thought I'd take a ride,
And soon Miss Fanny Bright
Was seated by my side;
The horse was lean and lank;
Misfortune seemed his lot;
He got into a drifted bank,
And then we got upsot.
(To Chorus:)

Verse 3:
A day or two ago,
The story I must tell,
I went out on the snow
And on my back I fell;
A gent was riding by
In a one-horse open sleigh,
He laughed as there I sprawling lie,
But quickly drove away.
(To Chorus:)

JOY TO THE WORLD

Words by
ISAAC WATTS

Music by
GEORGE F. HANDEL

MARCH OF THE TOYS

Bright march tempo

Music by
VICTOR HERBERT

Mandolin Solo:

March of the Toys - 2 - 1

March of the Toys - 2 - 2

O CHRISTMAS TREE
(O Tannenbaum)

OLD GERMAN CAROL

Moderate waltz

O Christmas Tree - 2 - 1

O Christmas Tree - 2 - 2

O COME, ALL YE FAITHFUL
(Adeste Fideles)

English Words by
FREDERICK OAKELEY
Latin Words Attributed to
JOHN FRANCIS WADE

Music by
JOHN READING

O Come, All Ye Faithful - 2 - 1

O COME, O COME EMMANUEL

TRADITIONAL

O Come, O Come Emmanuel - 3 - 1

Verse 3:
O come, Thou Day-Spring, come and cheer
Our spirits by Thine advent here;
Disperse the gloomy clouds of night,
And death's dark shadows put to fight.
(To Chorus:)

Verse 4:
O come, Thou Key of David, come,
And open wide our heav'nly home;
Make safe the way that leads on high,
And close the path to misery.
(To Chorus:)

Verse 5:
O come, O come, Thou Lord of might,
Who to Thy tribes, on Sinai's height,
In ancient times did'st give the law,
In cloud and majesty and awe.
(To Chorus:)

SILENT NIGHT

Words by
JOSEPH MOHR

Music by
FRANZ GRUBER

Moderately and gently

Lyrics:

1. Si - lent night, ho - ly night,
2. Si - lent night, ho - ly night,
3. Si - lent night, ho - ly night,

all   is   calm,   all   is   bright,
shep - herds   quake   at   the   sight.
Son   of   God,   love's   pure   light.

Silent Night - 3 - 1

O HOLY NIGHT

(Cantique de Noel)

Words and Music by
J. S. DWIGHT and ADOLPHE ADAM

Softly and slowly

O Holy Night - 4 - 1

O LITTLE TOWN OF BETHLEHEM

Words by
PHILLIPS BROOKS

Music by
LEWIS H. REDNER

O Little Town of Bethlehem - 2 - 2

PATAPAN

BURGUNDIAN CAROL

Patapan - 2 - 1

Verse 3:
God and man this day become
Joined as one with fife and drum.
Let the happy time play on,
Turelurelu, patapatapan.
Fife and drum together play,
As we sing on Christmas Day.

SIMPLE GIFTS

TRADITIONAL

Simple Gifts - 2 - 1

THE TWELVE DAYS OF CHRISTMAS

TRADITIONAL ENGLISH

The Twelve Days of Christmas - 8 - 2

88

The Twelve Days of Christmas - 8 - 3

Verse 9:

Verse 10:

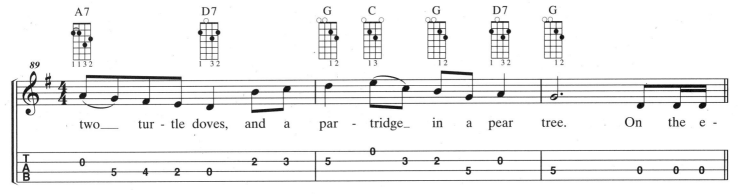

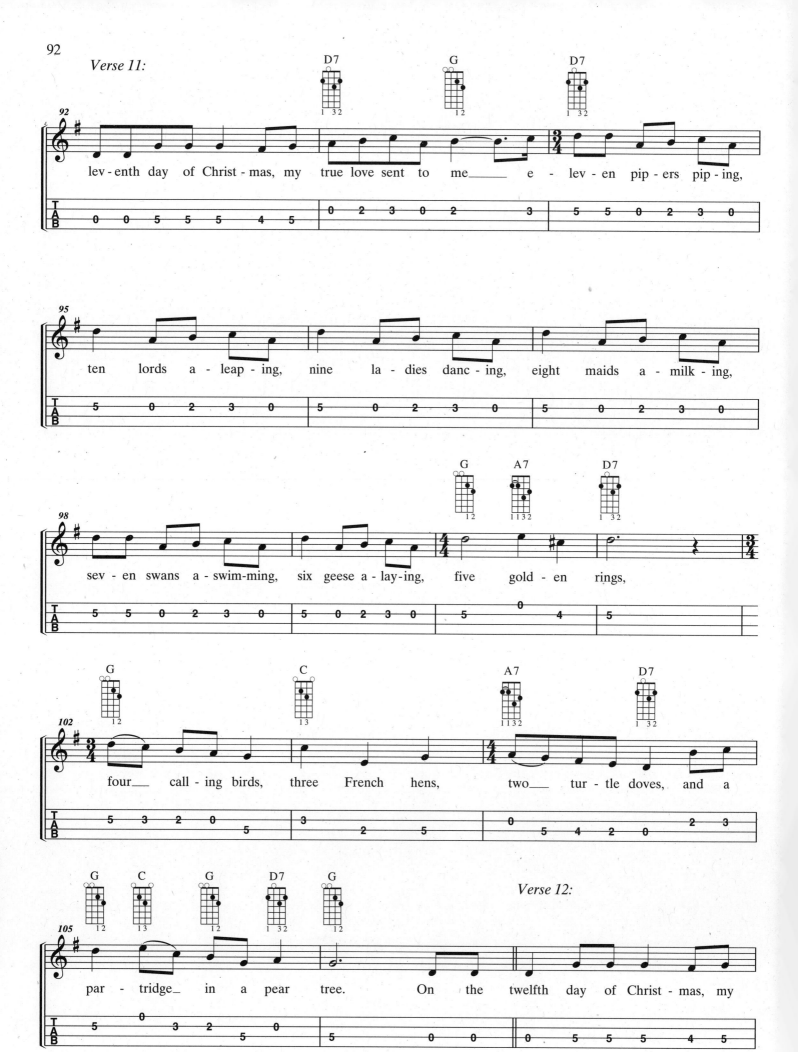

The Twelve Days of Christmas - 8 - 8

UKRAINIAN CAROL
(Carol of the Bells)

TRADITIONAL UKRAINIAN FOLK MELODY

Tempo ♩. = 60

Intro:

Verse:

Ukrainian Carol - 3 - 1

Ukrainian Carol - 3 - 2

WE THREE KINGS

Words and Music by
JOHN H. HOPKINS, JR.

bright,   west - ward   lead - ing,   still   pro - ceed - ing,

guide   us   to   Thy   per - fect   light.   light.

Verse 3:
Frankincense to offer have I,
Incense owns a deity nigh.
Prayer and praising, all men raising,
Worship Him, God most high.
(To Chorus:)

Verse 4:
Myrrh is mine: its bitter perfume
Breathes of life of gathering gloom;
Sorrowing, sighing, bleeding, dying,
Sealed in the stone cold tomb.
(To Chorus:)

Verse 5:
Glorious now behold Him arise;
King and God and sacrifice.
Alleluia, alleluia,
Earth to heaven replies.
(To Chorus:)

UP ON THE HOUSETOP

Words and Music by
BENJAMIN RUSSELL HANBY

WE WISH YOU A MERRY CHRISTMAS

TRADITIONAL ENGLISH FOLK SONG

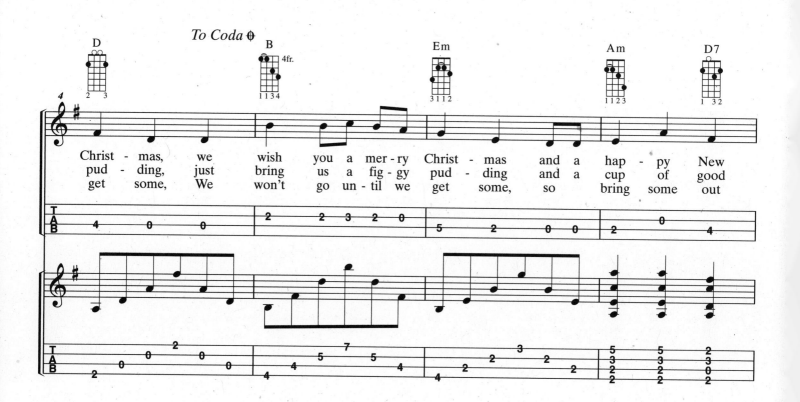

We Wish You a Merry Christmas - 2 - 2

WHAT CHILD IS THIS?

Based on
GREENSLEEVES,
an Old English Air
By
WILLIAM C. DIX

1. What child is this__ who laid to rest__ on Mar - y's lap__ is
2.3. *See additional lyrics*

sleep - ing? Whom an - gels greet__ with an - thems sweet,__ while shep - herds watch__ are

What Child Is This? - 2 - 1

Verse 2:
Why lies He in such mean estate,
Where ox and ass are feeding?
Good Christian, fear for sinners here,
The silent Word is pleading.
Nails, spears, shall pierce Him through,
The cross be borne for me, for you.
Hail, hail the Word made flesh,
The Babe, the Son of Mary!

Verse 3:
So bring Him incense, gold, and myrrh,
Come peasant, King to own Him;
The King of kings, salvation brings;
Let loving hearts enthrone Him.
Raise, raise the song on high,
The Virgin sings her lullaby.
Joy, joy, for Christ is born,
The Babe, the Son of Mary!

MANDOLIN CHORD DICTIONARY

A CHORDS

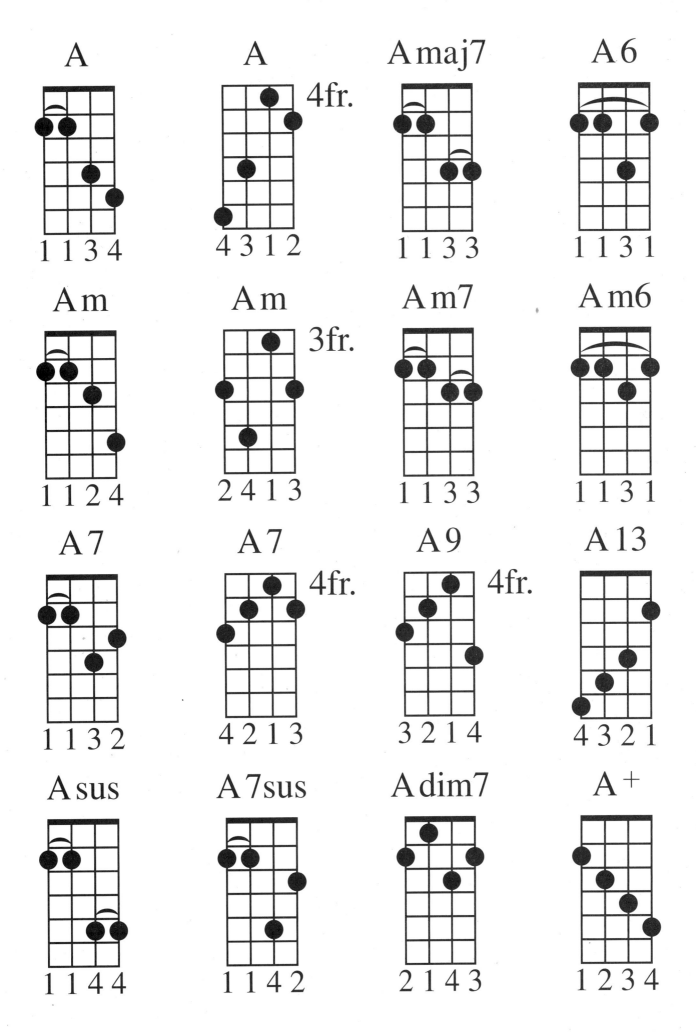

B♭ (A♯) CHORDS*

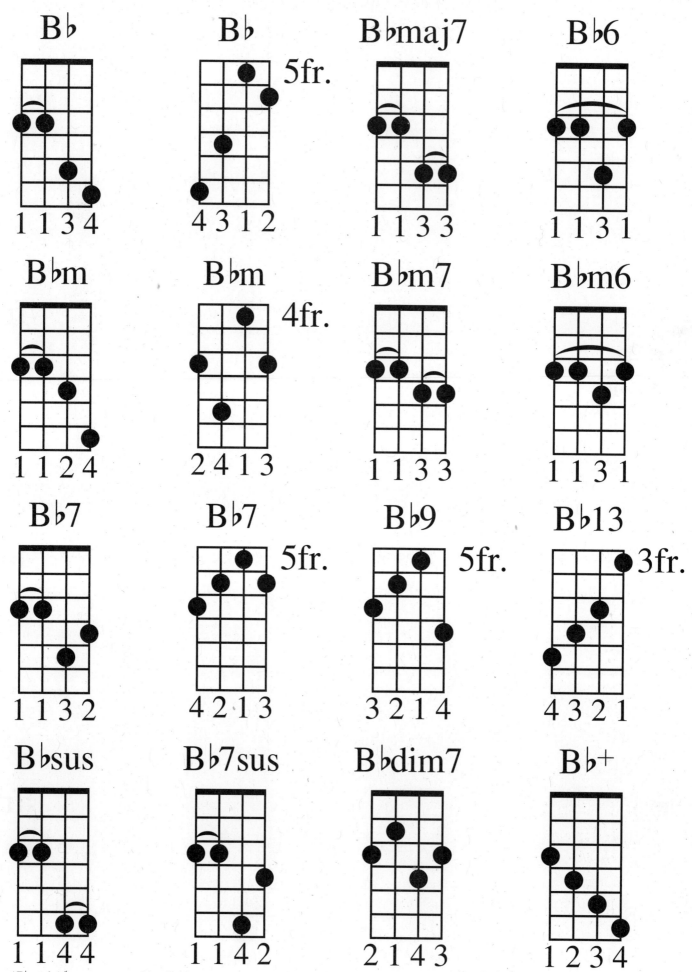

*B♭ and A♯ are two names for the same note.

B CHORDS

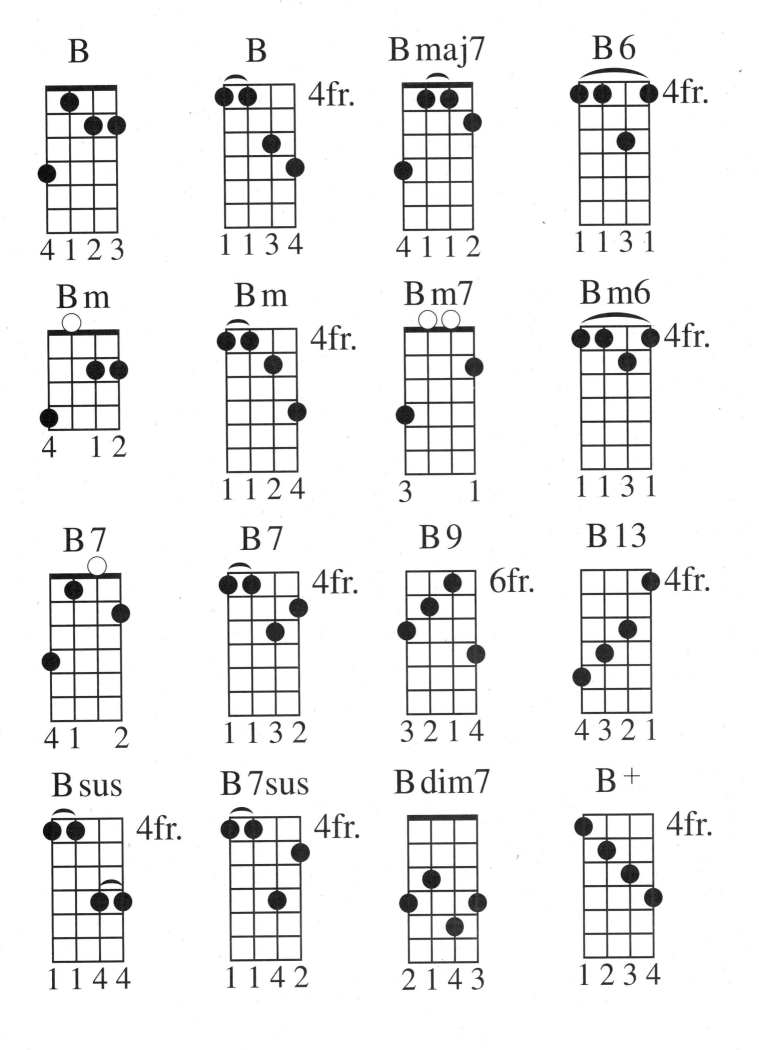

C CHORDS

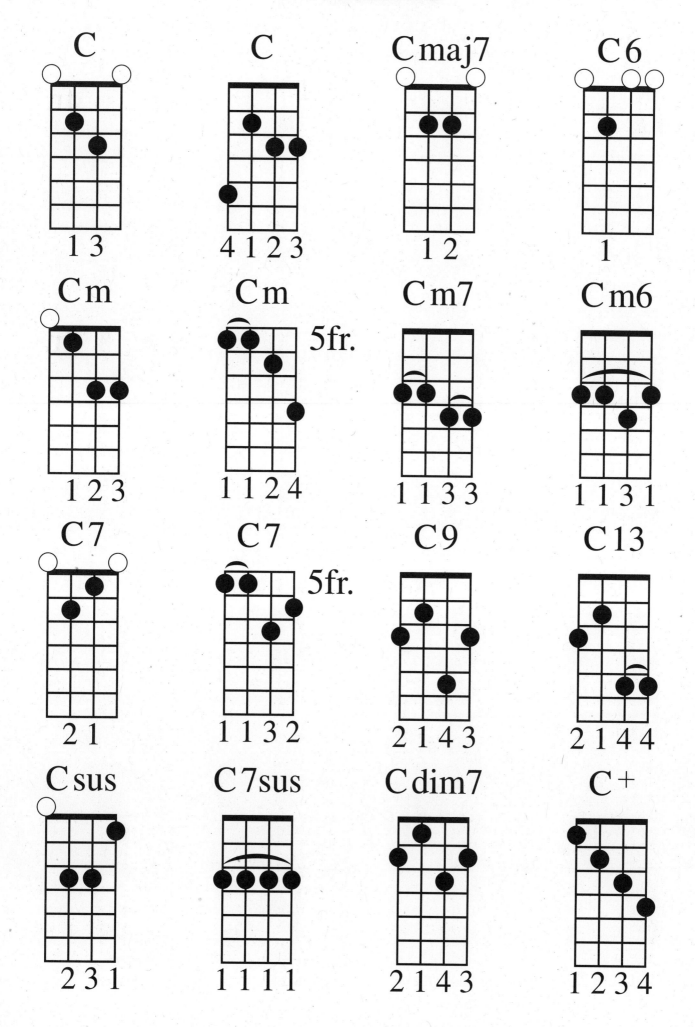

C♯ (D♭) CHORDS*

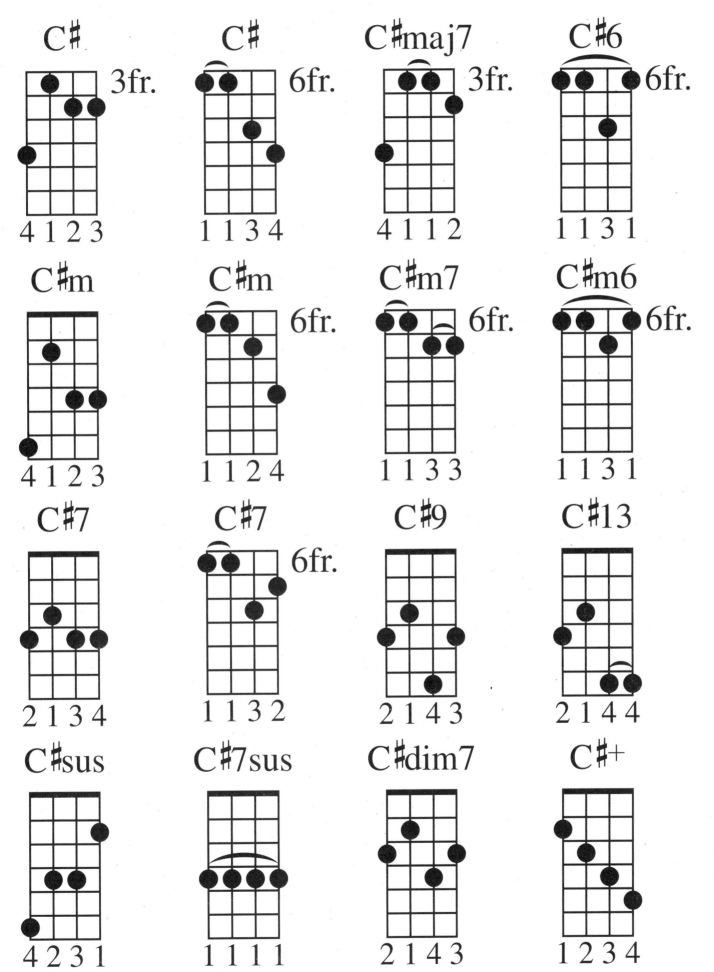

*C♯ and D♭ are two names for the same note.

D CHORDS

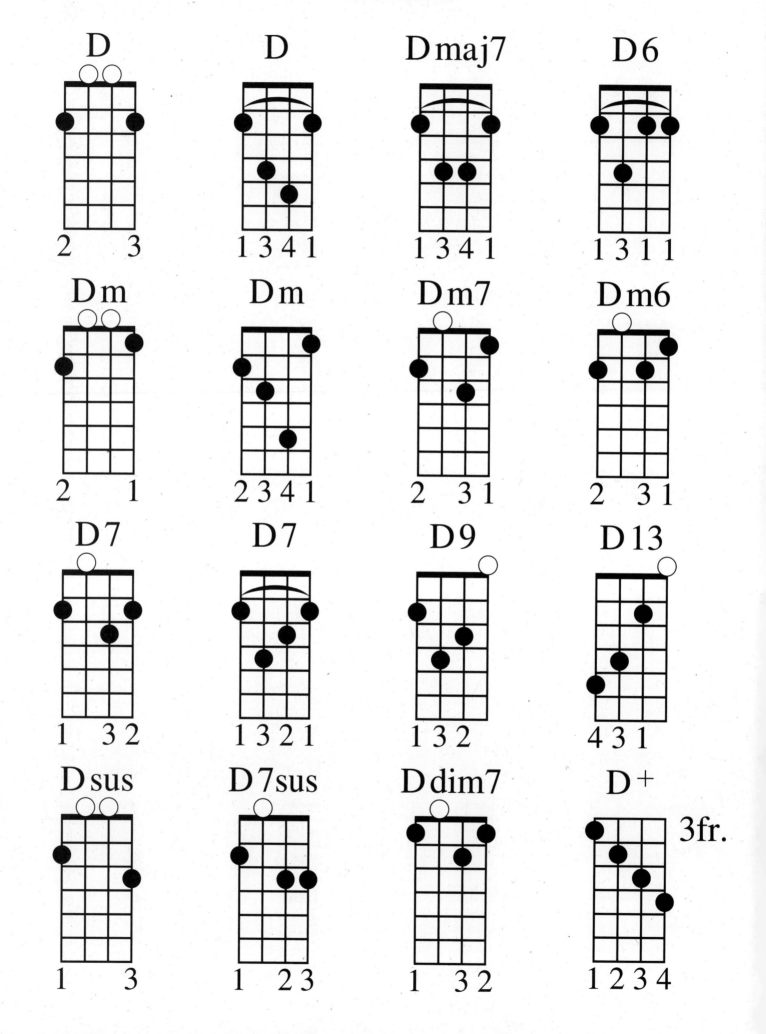

E♭ (D♯) CHORDS*

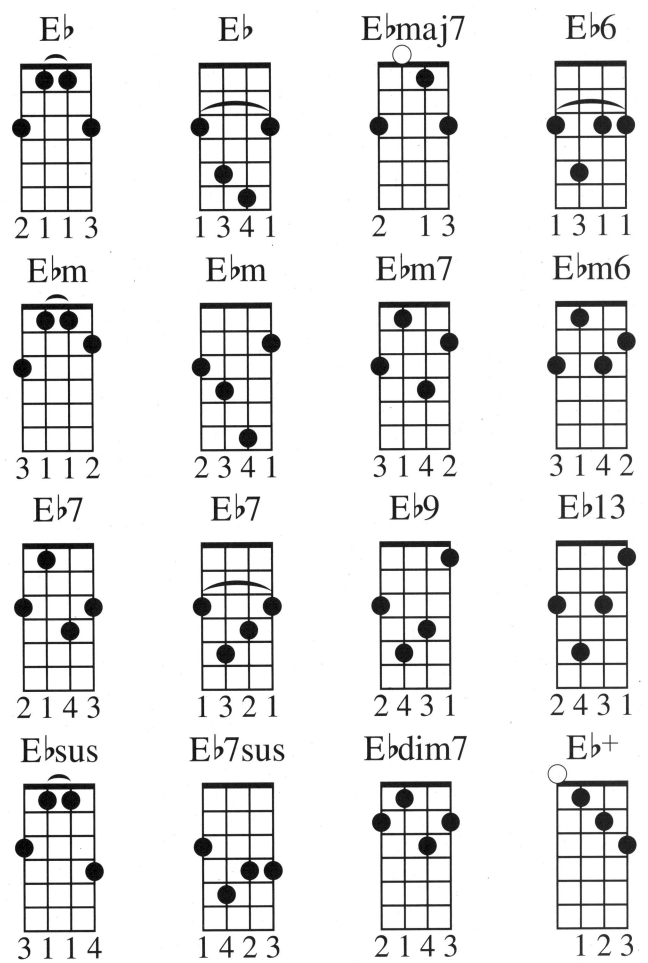

*E♭ and D♯ are two names for the same note.

E CHORDS

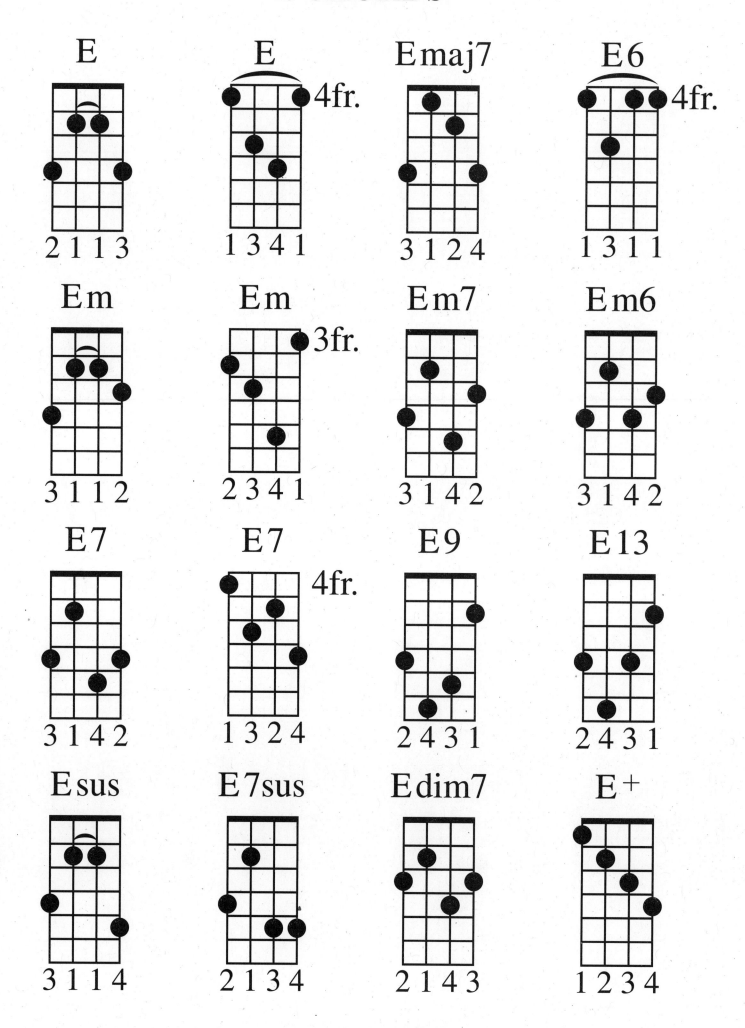

F CHORDS

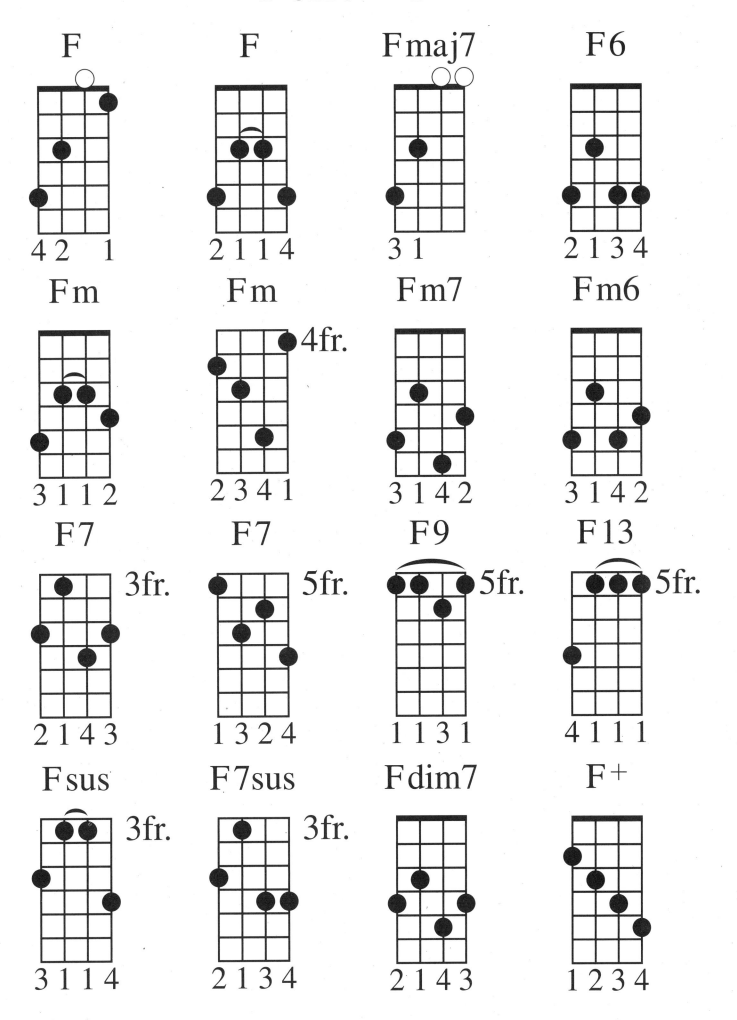

F# (G♭) CHORDS*

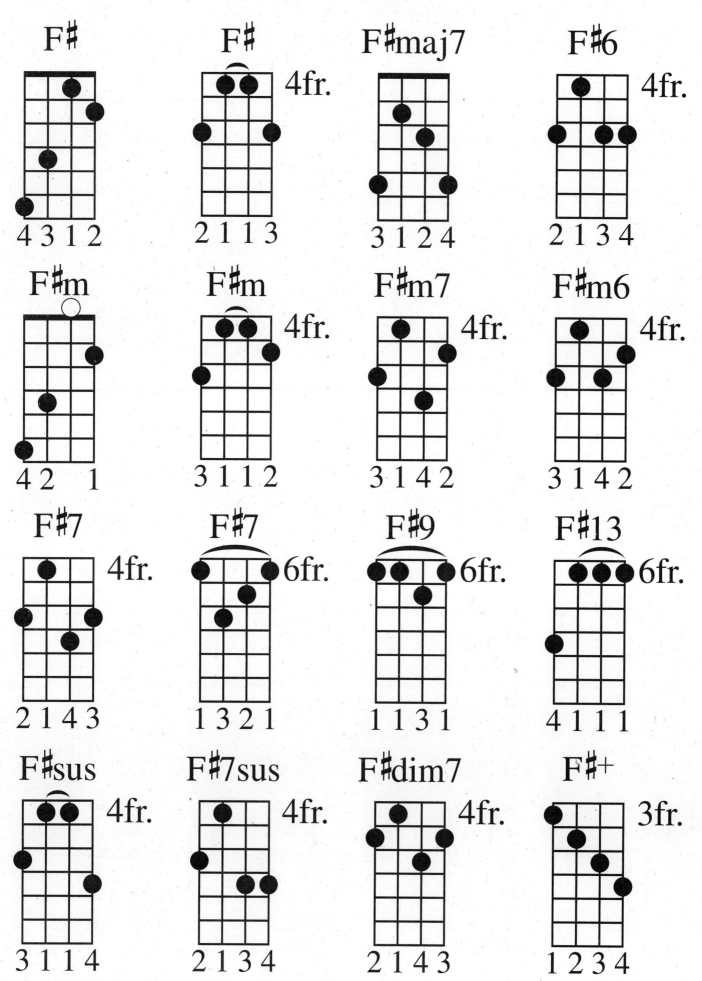

*F# and G♭ are two names for the same note.

G CHORDS

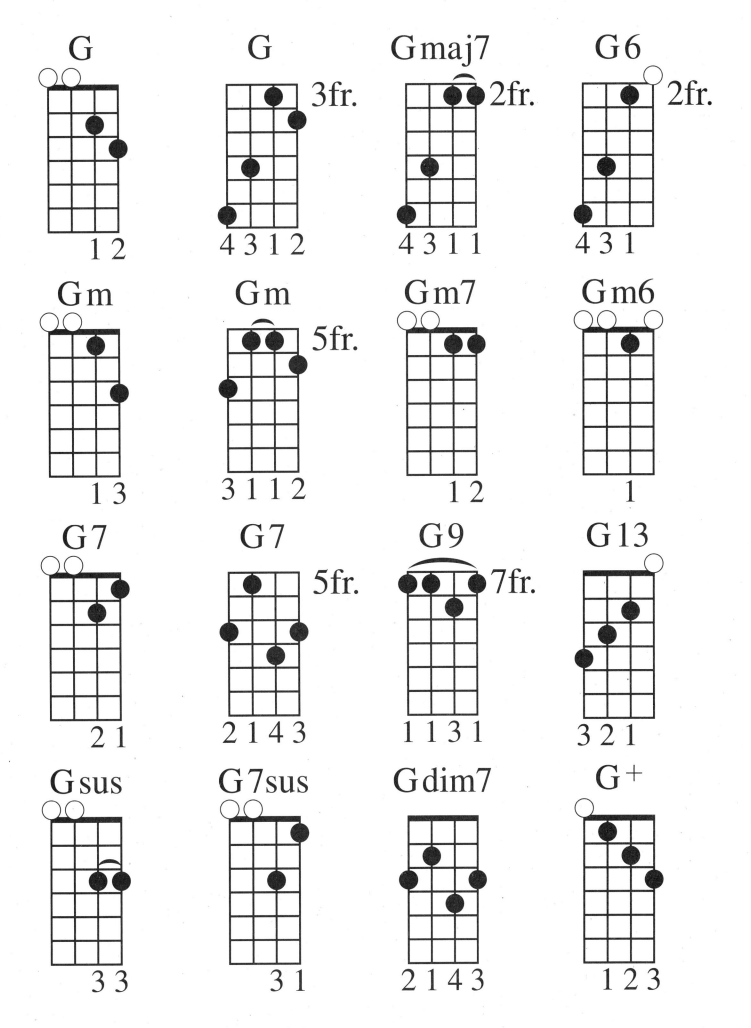

A♭ (G♯) CHORDS

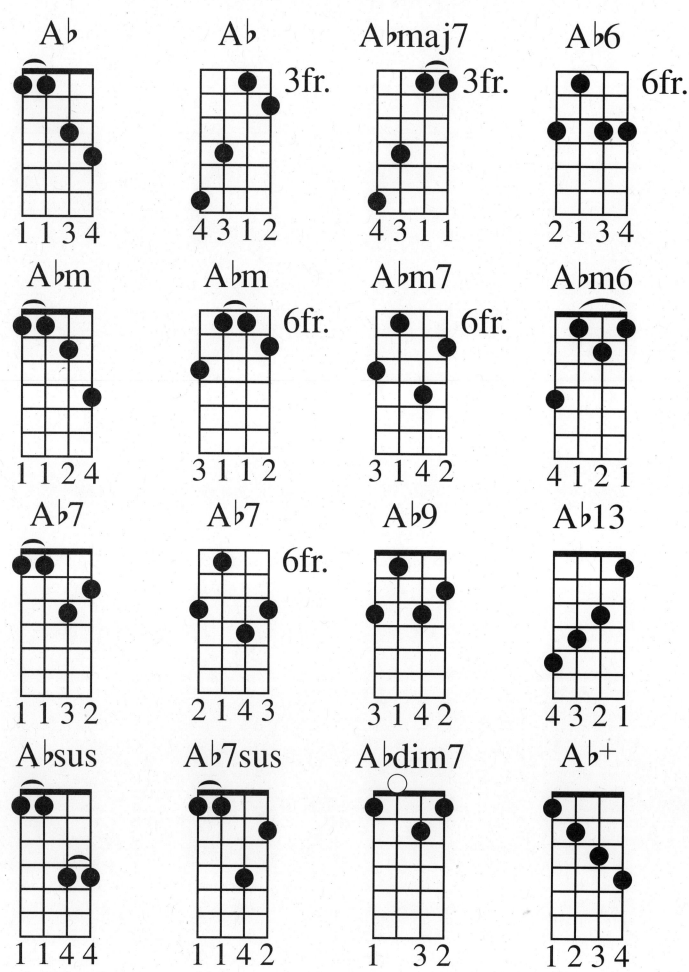

*A♭ and G♯ are two names for the same note.

JUST FOR FUN SERIES

The Just for Fun series is made up of 20 songbooks for guitar, ukulele, mandolin, and banjo. The books range in musical styles from swing and rock to pop and Christmas. All the arrangements are designed for the novice to intermediate player and feature authentic accompaniment parts and riffs. All books include TAB.

Classic Rock
Guitar............$14.99   00-33975
Ukulele..........$14.99   00-33976
Mandolin.......$14.99   00-33977
Banjo $14.99   00-33978

Swingin' Jazz
Guitar.............$14.99   00-33987
Ukulele..........$14.99   00-33988
Mandolin.......$14.99   00-33989
Banjo $14.99   00-33990

Easy Rock
Guitar.............$14.99   00-33979
Ukulele..........$14.99   00-33980
Mandolin.......$14.99   00-33981
Banjo $14.99   00-33982

Rock and Pop
Guitar.............$14.99   00-33983
Ukulele..........$14.99   00-33984
Mandolin.......$14.99   Q0-33985
Banjo $14.99   00-33986

Christmas Guitar
Easy Guitar TAB Edition
$16.99 00-35006

Christmas Ukulele
Easy Ukulele TAB Edition
$16.99 00-35007

Christmas Mandolin
Easy Mandolin TAB Edition
$16.99 00-35008

Christmas Banjo
Easy Banjo TAB Edition
$16.99 00-35009

AND MORE FOR UKULELE . . .

Uke 'An Play Rock
Ukulele TAB Edition
$19.95 00-30684

**Uke 'An Play
The Rolling Stones**
Ukulele TAB Edition
$19.99 00-34012

AVAILABLE at YOUR FAVORITE MUSIC RETAILER

Alfred Music Publishing
LEARN · TEACH · PLAY